CKD STAGE 4 COOKBOOK

FOR SENIORS

The Complete Guide With Recipes to Improve Renal Function and Help Manage Chronic Kidney Disease, Including 30 Day Meal Plan.

Joshua S. Gray

Table of Contents

SCAN THIS CODE TO GAIN ACCESS TO MORE BOOKS BY THE AUTHOR

INTRODUCTION

Have you ever wondered why managing Chronic Kidney Disease (CKD) Stage 4 seems like navigating a complex labyrinth of dietary restrictions and conflicting advice? Many people get caught up in a web of false beliefs about the most effective ways to support kidney function in their pursuit of optimal health. Well-meaning suggestions that a universal diet will solve all of the problems associated with Stage 4 CKD are frequently heard. However, what if I told you that the solutions that are frequently suggested may not be the panacea that people think they are?

CKD Stage 4 is a formidable health condition, and navigating its complexities can be both bewildering and overwhelming. The kidneys, responsible for filtering waste and excess fluids from the blood, face significant challenges at this stage. As a professional dietitian, I understand the struggles and concerns that often accompany a diagnosis of CKD Stage 4, and I am here to guide you through a journey towards improved well-being.

Just for a moment, consider the effects of having the information and resources necessary to not only survive but also thrive in spite of Stage 4 CKD. Imagine being in charge of your health again and adopting a way of life that feeds your body and soul. The CKD Stage 4 Cookbook For Seniors makes good on this promise.

You are about to go on the journey of discovery through the pages that follow, where you will come across a variety of information catered to your specific needs. This cookbook is a thorough guide created to address the particular dietary needs of CKD Stage 4, not just a compilation of recipes. It is a road map to a happier, healthier life where food serves as a useful tool to help you reach your goals of having the best possible kidney health rather than just being a source of nourishment.

I understand the difficulties you are facing, including the dietary limitations, the unpredictability, and the need for practical solutions. This cookbook is designed to tackle those issues head-on, with empathy and knowledge. You will obtain a thorough understanding of how to make tasty and well-informed decisions that promote kidney health by reading through its contents.

Come along on this life-changing adventure with me. As you embrace the specialized advice found within these pages, feel the anguish of uncertainty subside. Allow this cookbook to be the last word in addressing your dietary worries related to CKD Stage 4, opening the door to a future in which you will not only survive but thrive despite this health challenge.

Here's to your well-being and a delicious, kidney-friendly culinary adventure!

CHAPTER 1

Understanding Chronic Kidney Disease (CKD) Stage 4

Chronic Kidney Disease (CKD) is a progressive and potentially debilitating condition that affects millions of people worldwide. In the intricate landscape of CKD, Stage 4 marks a critical juncture where the kidneys face significant impairment in their ability to function optimally. To comprehend CKD Stage 4 thoroughly, it's crucial to delve into its causes, symptoms, and preventive measures.

Causes of CKD Stage 4

The journey to CKD Stage 4 often begins with underlying health conditions that contribute to the gradual decline in kidney function. Diabetes and hypertension stand out as primary culprits, relentlessly exerting pressure on the delicate filtration system of the kidneys. Other contributing factors include autoimmune diseases, genetic predispositions, and infections that target the kidneys.

As CKD progresses, the glomerular filtration rate (GFR), a key indicator of kidney function, declines to 15-29 milliliters per minute in Stage 4. The kidneys, responsible for filtering waste and excess fluids from the blood, struggle to maintain the delicate balance essential for overall health. Without timely intervention,

CKD can escalate to more advanced stages, leading to severe complications, including kidney failure.

Symptoms of CKD Stage 4

One of the challenges in managing CKD lies in its often subtle and insidious progression. In Stage 4, symptoms become more pronounced, reflecting the kidneys' compromised ability to carry out their essential functions. Fatigue, a consequence of anemia often associated with CKD, becomes a prevalent companion, sapping energy levels and diminishing the quality of life.

Fluid retention becomes apparent as the kidneys struggle to regulate water balance, leading to swelling in the legs and ankles. Elevated blood pressure, a common denominator in CKD, may become resistant to standard treatments at this stage. Additionally, individuals may experience changes in urine patterns, with alterations in color, frequency, and volume.

The accumulation of waste products in the blood can manifest in symptoms such as nausea, vomiting, and a metallic taste in the mouth. Bone health may also be compromised as the kidneys struggle to maintain the balance of calcium and phosphorus, leading to bone pain and an increased risk of fractures.

Preventive Measures

While CKD Stage 4 presents formidable challenges, a proactive approach to preventive measures can significantly impact the trajectory of the disease. Education and awareness play a pivotal role in empowering individuals to make informed lifestyle choices that safeguard kidney health.

1. **Manage Underlying Conditions:** Addressing conditions like diabetes and hypertension is paramount. Consistent monitoring and management, often through medication, lifestyle modifications, and regular check-ups, can help slow the progression of CKD.

2.   Maintain a Healthy Diet: Dietary choices wield considerable influence over kidney health. A diet rich in fruits, vegetables, whole grains, and lean proteins can support overall well-being. However, in CKD Stage 4, specific dietary adjustments, such as limiting phosphorus and potassium intake, become crucial.

3.   Stay Hydrated: Adequate hydration is essential for kidney function. Striking the right balance ensures that the kidneys can efficiently filter waste products. However, individuals with CKD should be mindful of fluid intake, as excessive fluids can contribute to swelling and hypertension.

4.   Regular Exercise: Physical activity promotes cardiovascular health and helps manage conditions like diabetes and hypertension. Tailoring exercise routines to individual capabilities is crucial, and consultation with healthcare professionals can provide guidance on safe and effective exercises.

5. **Medication Adherence:** Following prescribed medications diligently is crucial in managing CKD. Medications may include those to control blood pressure, manage diabetes, or address specific symptoms associated with Stage 4 CKD. Regular communication with healthcare providers ensures adjustments to medication plans as needed.

6. **Regular Monitoring:** Routine check-ups and monitoring of kidney function are essential components of preventive care. Regular assessments of GFR, blood pressure, and other relevant markers allow healthcare

providers to intervene promptly and adjust treatment plans as needed.

7. **Quit Smoking and Limit Alcohol:** Smoking and excessive alcohol consumption can exacerbate the progression of CKD. Quitting smoking and moderating alcohol intake contribute positively to overall health and support kidney function.

In essence, preventive measures revolve around a holistic and proactive approach to health. By embracing lifestyle changes, adhering to prescribed treatments, and fostering open communication with healthcare providers, individuals can exert a positive influence on the course of CKD Stage 4.

CHAPTER 2

Foods to Embrace and Avoid for Optimum Health

Chronic Kidney Disease (CKD) Stage 4 necessitates a meticulous approach to diet, as the kidneys, already compromised in their function, require support in managing waste and fluid balance. A well-designed CKD Stage 4 diet aims to optimize health by selecting foods that alleviate the burden on the kidneys while avoiding those that can exacerbate the condition. Let's explore the key principles of a CKD Stage 4 diet, highlighting foods to embrace and avoid for optimum health.

Foods to Embrace

1.   **Lean Proteins:** Opt for high-quality, lean protein sources such as poultry, fish, and eggs. These proteins provide essential amino acids without burdening the kidneys with excessive waste products.

2.   **Fruits and Vegetables:** Incorporate a variety of fruits and vegetables into your diet for their rich antioxidant content and essential vitamins. However, be mindful of potassium levels; choose lower-potassium options like berries, apples, and cauliflower.

3.   **Whole Grains:** Whole grains such as brown rice, quinoa, and whole wheat products offer fiber and essential nutrients without contributing to excessive phosphorus levels.

4. **Healthy Fats:** Include sources of healthy fats, such as avocados, olive oil, and fatty fish like salmon. These fats support overall health without imposing additional stress on the kidneys.

5. **Low-Phosphorus Dairy:** Dairy can be part of a CKD Stage 4 diet, but choose low-phosphorus options like cream cheese, butter, and limited quantities of milk. Monitor phosphorus intake, as high levels can contribute to bone health issues.

6. **Herbs and Spices:** Flavor your meals with herbs and spices to enhance taste without relying on excessive salt. Managing sodium intake is crucial for controlling blood pressure and fluid balance.

7. **Egg Whites:** Egg whites are a protein-rich option without the phosphorus content found in egg yolks. Incorporate them into your diet for a kidney-friendly protein source.

Foods to Avoid

1.   **High-Potassium   Foods:**   Limit high-potassium foods like bananas, oranges, tomatoes, and potatoes. Elevated potassium levels can pose a risk for individuals with compromised kidney function.

2.   **Phosphorus-Rich Foods:** Reduce intake of phosphorus-rich foods such as dairy products, nuts, seeds, and whole grains. Elevated phosphorus can contribute to bone and cardiovascular issues in CKD Stage 4.

3.   **Processed   Foods:**   Processed and packaged foods often contain high levels of sodium, additives, and preservatives. These can contribute to hypertension and fluid retention, which are concerns for individuals with CKD.

4.   **Red and Processed Meats:** Red meats and processed meats are high in phosphorus and should be limited in a CKD Stage 4 diet. Opt for lean protein sources to minimize the impact on kidney function.

5.   **Caffeine and Carbonated Beverages:** Excessive consumption of caffeine and carbonated beverages can lead to dehydration and disrupt fluid balance. Choose water as the primary hydrating beverage.

6.   **Certain Vegetables:** While vegetables are generally encouraged, some high-potassium choices like spinach and kale should be consumed in moderation. Cooking methods, such as boiling, can reduce potassium levels in vegetables.

7.   **High-Sodium Foods:** Minimize intake of high-sodium foods, including processed snacks, canned soups, and fast food. Monitoring sodium is essential for managing blood pressure and fluid retention.

A CKD Stage 4 diet requires careful planning and individualization. Regular consultation with a registered dietitian is paramount to tailor dietary recommendations based on specific health needs and preferences. Additionally, staying hydrated within recommended limits and maintaining a balanced, kidney-friendly diet can contribute significantly to overall well-being.

Benefits of Following CKD Stage 4 Diet For Seniors

Chronic Kidney Disease (CKD) Stage 4 is characterized by a significant reduction in kidney function, with a glomerular filtration rate (GFR) ranging from 15 to 29 ml/min per 1.73 m². Following a CKD Stage 4 diet is crucial for seniors to manage symptoms, slow down the progression of the disease, and maintain overall health. Here are some core benefits of adhering to a CKD Stage 4 diet for seniors:

1. Fluid Management:

Kidneys play a key role in regulating fluid balance. In CKD Stage 4, the kidneys struggle to efficiently eliminate excess fluids. Following a restricted fluid intake helps prevent fluid overload, swelling, and high blood pressure.

2. Protein Restriction:

The kidneys may struggle to eliminate waste products from protein metabolism. A controlled protein intake helps manage the buildup of waste products, such as urea and creatinine, in the blood, reducing the burden on the kidneys.

3. Phosphorus Control:

With impaired kidney function, phosphorus levels can become elevated, leading to bone and cardiovascular complications. A CKD Stage 4 diet typically involves limiting phosphorus-rich foods to maintain a healthy balance.

4. Sodium (Salt) Restriction:

High blood pressure is a common complication in CKD, and limiting sodium intake helps control blood pressure. Reducing salt intake is essential to manage fluid retention and decrease the risk of cardiovascular events.

5. Potassium Management:

As kidney function declines, the body may struggle to regulate potassium levels. Too much potassium can lead to dangerous heart arrhythmias. A CKD Stage 4 diet often involves monitoring and limiting potassium-rich foods.

6. Caloric Intake and Weight Management:

Maintaining a healthy weight is crucial for seniors with CKD. A CKD Stage 4 diet provides an appropriate caloric intake while addressing specific nutrient needs, helping to prevent malnutrition and supporting overall well-being.

7. Blood Sugar Control (for Diabetic Patients):

Many seniors with CKD also have diabetes. Controlling blood sugar levels through diet is essential for managing diabetes and preventing further kidney damage.

8. Vitamin and Mineral Supplementation:

Due to dietary restrictions, seniors may be at risk of vitamin and mineral deficiencies. Supplementation may be recommended to ensure they receive essential nutrients without exacerbating kidney-related issues.

9. Individualized Nutrition Plan:

Each individual may have unique dietary needs and restrictions. Working with a registered dietitian or healthcare professional helps tailor a CKD Stage 4 diet to the specific requirements and preferences of the senior, optimizing nutrition while managing kidney function.

10. Symptom Management and Quality of Life:

Following a CKD Stage 4 diet can help alleviate symptoms associated with advanced kidney disease, such as fatigue, nausea, and loss of appetite. Improving the overall nutritional status contributes to a better quality of life for seniors with CKD.

How to Follow a CKD Stage 4 Diet

1. Consult a Healthcare Professional:

Before making any significant dietary changes, consult with a healthcare team, including a nephrologist and a registered dietitian who specializes in renal nutrition. They will assess your specific condition and provide personalized recommendations.

2. Protein Restriction:

Limit protein intake to manage the accumulation of waste products from protein metabolism. High-quality proteins from sources such as poultry, fish, and eggs may be recommended in moderation. Plant-based protein sources may also be considered.

3. Phosphorus Control:

Reduce phosphorus intake by avoiding high-phosphorus foods, such as dairy products, nuts, seeds, and certain processed foods. Phosphorus binders may be prescribed to help control phosphorus levels.

4. Sodium (Salt) Restriction:

Limit sodium intake to control blood pressure and fluid retention. Avoid processed and canned foods, and use herbs and spices for flavoring instead of salt. Read food labels for sodium content.

5. Potassium Management:

Monitor and limit potassium-rich foods, such as bananas, oranges, tomatoes, and potatoes. Cooking methods like boiling or leaching can help reduce potassium content in certain vegetables.

6. Fluid Management:

Follow a prescribed fluid restriction to prevent fluid overload. Monitor fluid intake from all sources, including beverages and moist foods like soup and fruits. Be mindful of excessive thirst and fluid retention symptoms.

7. Caloric Intake and Weight Management:

Maintain a healthy weight through portion control and a balanced diet. A dietitian can help determine the appropriate caloric intake based on individual needs and activity levels.

8. Blood Sugar Control (for Diabetic Patients):

If you have diabetes, manage blood sugar levels through dietary changes, medication, and insulin as prescribed by your healthcare team.

9. Vitamin and Mineral Supplementation:

Take prescribed vitamin and mineral supplements, if necessary, to prevent deficiencies. Common supplements include calcium, vitamin D, and iron. However, supplementation should be guided by healthcare professionals to avoid overconsumption.

10. Individualized Nutrition Plan:

Work with a registered dietitian to develop an individualized nutrition plan that considers personal preferences, cultural factors, and specific health needs. Regular monitoring and adjustments to the diet plan may be necessary.

11. Symptom Management:

Address symptoms such as fatigue, nausea, and loss of appetite through dietary modifications. Smaller, more frequent meals and changes in food preparation methods can help improve overall nutrition and well-being.

12. Monitor Laboratory Values:

Regularly monitor kidney function and other relevant laboratory values to assess the effectiveness of the diet plan. Adjustments to the diet may be needed based on changes in these values.

CHAPTER 3

Shopping List

When shopping for a CKD Stage 4 diet, it's important to choose foods that align with the dietary restrictions and guidelines for managing advanced chronic kidney disease. Here is a list of ingredients or items that can be included in a CKD Stage 4 diet:

1. Low-Phosphorus Proteins:

- Skinless poultry (chicken, turkey)

- Fish (low in phosphorus, such as salmon, trout, and flounder)

- Eggs (limit yolks)

2. Low-Potassium Fruits:

- Apples

- Berries (strawberries, blueberries)

- Pineapple (in moderation)

- Canned peaches or pears (in juice, not syrup)

3. Low-Potassium Vegetables:

- Cauliflower

- Cabbage

- Bell peppers

- Green beans

4. Low-Sodium Grains and Starches:

- White rice

- White bread

- Pasta (limit intake)

- Cornflakes or rice cereals (low sodium)

5. Low-Phosphorus Dairy Alternatives:

- Unenriched rice milk

- Unenriched almond milk

- Low-phosphorus creamers

6. Cooking Oils:

- Olive oil

- Canola oil

7. Herbs and Spices (Salt Alternatives):

- Garlic powder

- Onion powder

- Basil

- Cilantro

- Turmeric

8. Low-Phosphorus Snacks:

- Unsalted popcorn

- Rice cakes

- Hard candies (avoid those with phosphate additives)

9. Beverages:

- Water (in accordance with fluid restrictions)
- Herbal teas (avoid high-potassium blends)
- Lemonade (homemade, controlling potassium content)

10. Low-Potassium Desserts:

- Sorbet
- Sherbet
- Angel food cake

11. Protein Supplements (if needed):

- Low-phosphorus protein powders or supplements (under the guidance of a healthcare professional)

12. Low-Phosphorus Condiments:

- Vinegar

- Mustard

- Ketchup (in moderation)

13. Canned Vegetables (Choose Low-Potassium Varieties):

- Green beans

- Carrots

14. Low-Phosphorus Cereal:

- Cornflakes

- Puffed rice cereal

15. Low-Potassium Sweeteners:

- Honey

- Maple syrup

16. Low-Phosphorus Nuts and Seeds (in moderation):

- Almonds (limited quantity)
- Pine nuts
- Sunflower seeds

17. Low-Sodium Broths:

- Chicken or vegetable broth (check labels for sodium content)

18. Non-Dairy Creamer Alternatives:

- Rice milk-based creamer
- Almond milk-based creamer

19. Low-Phosphorus Pasta Alternatives:

- Egg noodles
- Rice noodles

20. Fresh Herbs and Citrus:

- Parsley

- Cilantro

- Lemon or lime (for flavoring)

When shopping for a CKD Stage 4 diet, it's essential to read food labels carefully, paying attention to the phosphorus, potassium, and sodium content.

Complications of CKD Stage 4

If the right diet is not adopted in CKD Stage 4, several complications can arise, potentially accelerating the progression of kidney disease and negatively impacting overall health. Here are some of the potential complications:

1. Fluid Overload:

Without proper fluid management, individuals with CKD Stage 4 may experience fluid retention, leading to swelling (edema), high blood pressure, and an increased risk of heart failure.

2. Electrolyte Imbalances:

Inadequate control of potassium, phosphorus, and sodium intake can result in electrolyte imbalances. High levels of potassium (hyperkalemia), phosphorus (hyperphosphatemia), and sodium (hypernatremia) can lead to various complications, including cardiac arrhythmias and bone disorders.

3. Worsening Kidney Function:

A diet that is not tailored to CKD Stage 4 can contribute to further deterioration of kidney function. Increased workload on already compromised kidneys due to excessive protein intake or other dietary factors may accelerate the decline in glomerular filtration rate (GFR).

4. Cardiovascular Complications:

Chronic kidney disease is closely associated with an increased risk of cardiovascular disease. Poorly managed diet can contribute to hypertension, dyslipidemia, and inflammation, increasing the risk of heart attacks, strokes, and other cardiovascular events.

5. Anemia:

Inadequate iron intake or impaired absorption can lead to anemia, a common complication in CKD. Anemia can result in fatigue, weakness, and reduced oxygen-carrying capacity in the blood.

6. Malnutrition:

Inappropriate dietary choices or restrictions can lead to malnutrition. Malnourished individuals may experience weight loss, muscle wasting, and a weakened immune system, compromising overall health.

7. Bone Disorders:

Elevated phosphorus levels can contribute to bone disorders, including renal osteodystrophy. This condition involves abnormalities in bone mineralization, leading to weakened bones, fractures, and joint pain.

8. Metabolic Acidosis:

CKD can impair the kidneys' ability to excrete acids, leading to metabolic acidosis. This condition can result in muscle wasting, bone demineralization, and impaired organ function.

9. Compromised Immune Function:

Poor nutrition and electrolyte imbalances can weaken the immune system, making individuals more susceptible to infections. Infections can further stress the kidneys and contribute to complications.

10. Decreased Quality of Life:

The combination of physical symptoms, complications, and the impact on daily life can significantly reduce the quality of life for individuals with CKD Stage 4 who do not adhere to a suitable diet. Fatigue, nausea, and other symptoms can make it challenging to engage in regular activities.

CHAPTER 4

Meal Planning For CKD Stage 4

Meal planning for a CKD Stage 4 diet involves creating well-balanced and individualized meal plans to manage symptoms, slow the progression of chronic kidney disease, and improve overall health. Here are some key aspects of meal planning for CKD Stage 4, along with the benefits it offers for proper management:

Key Aspects of CKD Stage 4 Meal Planning:

1. Protein Management:

Proper protein management helps control the buildup of waste products in the blood. Restricting high-phosphorus proteins and opting for moderate amounts of high-quality protein sources, such as poultry and fish, can be beneficial.

2. Phosphorus Control:

Limiting phosphorus intake helps prevent complications such as bone disorders and cardiovascular issues. Choosing low-phosphorus foods and avoiding processed foods with phosphorus additives is crucial.

3. Potassium Monitoring:

Controlling potassium intake helps prevent hyperkalemia, which can lead to dangerous heart arrhythmias. Identifying and limiting high-potassium foods is important in meal planning.

4. Sodium Restriction:

Managing sodium intake is essential for controlling blood pressure and preventing fluid retention. Choosing fresh, whole foods and avoiding processed or canned items with high sodium content supports overall kidney health.

5. Fluid Management:

Adhering to prescribed fluid restrictions helps prevent fluid overload, swelling, and hypertension. Monitoring fluid intake from both beverages and foods contributes to effective fluid management.

6. Caloric and Weight Control:

Maintaining a healthy weight is crucial for managing CKD Stage 4. Balanced caloric intake supports overall well-being and prevents malnutrition, especially in individuals with decreased appetite.

7. Individualized Nutrition Plans:

Every individual with CKD Stage 4 has unique dietary needs. Working with a registered dietitian to create an individualized nutrition plan ensures that the diet addresses specific requirements, preferences, and cultural considerations.

8. Monitoring Blood Sugar (for Diabetic Patients):

Individuals with both CKD and diabetes need careful management of blood sugar levels. Meal planning involves controlling carbohydrate intake and choosing low-glycemic foods to prevent further kidney damage.

9. Vitamin and Mineral Supplementation:

Meal planning may include the use of vitamin and mineral supplements to address potential deficiencies. This helps maintain overall health while adhering to dietary restrictions.

Benefits of Proper Meal Planning for CKD Stage 4

1. Disease Progression Control:

Properly planned meals can slow the progression of CKD Stage 4 by managing key nutritional elements, reducing the workload on the kidneys, and preventing complications.

2. Symptom Management:

Well-balanced meals can help alleviate symptoms such as fatigue, nausea, and loss of appetite commonly associated with advanced kidney disease.

3. Improved Nutritional Status:

Adequate nutrition supports overall health and helps prevent malnutrition. This is particularly important as individuals with CKD may face challenges in obtaining essential nutrients.

4. Enhanced Quality of Life:

A carefully planned CKD Stage 4 diet can contribute to an improved quality of life by minimizing symptoms, reducing the risk of complications, and supporting overall well-being.

5. Individualized Approach:

Tailoring meal plans to individual needs ensures that dietary recommendations are realistic, achievable, and align with personal preferences, promoting long-term adherence.

6. Prevention of Complications:

By addressing specific dietary concerns, such as phosphorus and potassium control, meal planning helps prevent complications such as bone disorders, electrolyte imbalances, and cardiovascular issues.

7. Collaboration with Healthcare Professionals:

Working closely with a healthcare team, including nephrologists and dietitians, during meal planning ensures that dietary recommendations align with medical management and are regularly adjusted based on changing health conditions.

8. Empowerment and Education:

Meal planning empowers individuals to take an active role in managing their health. Education about food choices, portion control, and cooking methods fosters a sense of control and responsibility.

CHAPTER 5

Breakfast Recipes

1. Burrito with Turkey

Ingredients:

- 1 whole wheat tortilla

- 75g lean ground turkey

- ¼ cup diced tomatoes

- 2 tablespoons diced onions

- ¼ cup shredded lettuce

- 1 tablespoon low-phosphorus salsa

Preparation:

1. In a non-stick skillet, cook the ground turkey until fully cooked.

2. Warm the whole wheat tortilla.

3. Assemble the burrito by placing the cooked turkey, diced tomatoes, onions, lettuce, and salsa in the center of the tortilla.

4. Fold the sides of the tortilla and roll it up.

Nutritional Value:

- Protein: 15g

- Phosphorus: < 150mg

- Potassium: < 200mg

- Sodium: < 200mg

Cooking Time:

Approximately 15 minutes.

2. Easy Pancakes with Fresh Fruit

Ingredients:

- ½ cup pancake mix (low-phosphorus)
- 1/3 cup water
- ½ cup fresh berries (blueberries, strawberries)

Preparation:

1. Mix the pancake mix with water until smooth.

2. Heat a non-stick pan and pour small amounts of batter to make pancakes.

3. Cook until surface bubbles appear, then turn and continue cooking on the other side.

4. Top with fresh berries.

Nutritional Value:

- Protein: 5g

- Phosphorus: < 100mg

- Potassium: < 100mg

- Sodium: < 100mg

Cooking Time:

Approximately 15 minutes.

3. Baked Eggs with Veggies

Ingredients:

- 2 eggs
- ¼ cup diced bell peppers
- ¼ cup diced zucchini
- 1 tablespoon chopped parsley
- Salt and pepper to taste

Preparation:

1. Preheat the oven to 375°F (190°C).

2. Grease a baking dish.

3. Crack the eggs into the dish and surround them with diced vegetables.

4. Season with salt and pepper.

5. Bake until the egg whites are set but the yolks are still runny or to your preference.

Nutritional Value:

- Protein: 12g

- Phosphorus: < 150mg

- Potassium: < 200mg

- Sodium: < 100mg

Cooking Time:

Approximately 12-15 minutes.

4. Toast with Avocado and Eggs

Ingredients:

- 1 slice whole grain bread
- ¼ avocado, mashed
- 1 poached or fried egg
- Salt and pepper to taste

Preparation:

1. Toast the bread.
2. Spread mashed avocado on the toast.
3. Top with a poached or fried egg.
4. Season with salt and pepper.

Nutritional Value:

- Protein: 10g

- Phosphorus: < 100mg

- Potassium: < 150mg

- Sodium: < 100mg

Cooking Time:

Approximately 10 minutes.

5. Fresh Fruit Salad

Ingredients:

- ½ cup diced melons (cantaloupe, honeydew)
- ½ cup diced berries (strawberries, blueberries)
- ½ cup diced pineapple
- 1 tablespoon fresh mint, chopped

Preparation:

1. Mix all the diced fruits in a bowl.
2. Garnish with fresh mint.

Nutritional Value:

- Protein: 1g
- Phosphorus: < 50mg
- Potassium: < 200mg
- Sodium: < 5mg

Cooking Time:

No cooking required.

6.   Filled Cookies

Ingredients:

- 2 low-phosphorus cookies
- 1 tablespoon almond butter (unsalted)
- 1 teaspoon honey

Preparation:

1. Spread almond butter on one side of each cookie.

2. Drizzle honey over the almond butter on one cookie.

3. Place the other cookie on top to make a sandwich.

Nutritional Value:

- Protein: 4g

- Phosphorus: < 50mg

- Potassium: < 50mg

- Sodium: < 50mg

Cooking Time:

No cooking required.

7. Quick and Tasty Chocolate Banana Oatmeal

- ½ cup rolled oats
- 1 cup water or low-phosphorus milk
- ½ ripe banana, mashed
- 1 tablespoon unsweetened cocoa powder
- 1 teaspoon honey (optional)

Preparation:

1. Cook oats with water or milk according to package instructions.
2. Stir in mashed banana and cocoa powder.
3. Sweeten with honey if desired.

Nutritional Value:

- Protein: 5g

- Phosphorus: < 100mg

- Potassium: < 150mg

- Sodium: < 50mg

Cooking Time:

Approximately 5-7 minutes.

8. Toast with Figs and Cottage Cheese

Ingredients:

- 1 slice whole grain bread
- 2 tablespoons low-fat cottage cheese
- 2-3 fresh figs, sliced
- 1 teaspoon honey

Preparation:

1. Toast the bread.
2. Spread cottage cheese on the toast.
3. Top with sliced figs.
4. Drizzle with honey.

Nutritional Value:

- Protein: 7g

- Phosphorus: < 100mg

- Potassium: < 150mg

- Sodium: < 100mg

Cooking Time:

Approximately 5 minutes.

9. Blueberry and Oat Cake

Ingredients:

- ¼ cup rolled oats

- ¼ cup blueberries (fresh or frozen)

- 1 tablespoon almond flour

- 1 tablespoon unsweetened applesauce

- ¼ teaspoon baking powder

- 1 teaspoon honey

Preparation:

1. Mix all ingredients in a microwave-safe mug.

2. Microwave on high for 2-3 minutes until the cake is set.

3. Allow to cool before eating.

Nutritional Value:

- Protein: 5g

- Phosphorus: < 100mg

- Potassium: < 50mg

- Sodium: < 50mg

Cooking Time:

Approximately 3 minutes.

10. Eggs with Parmesan Cheese

- 2 eggs
- 1 tablespoon grated Parmesan cheese
- Salt and pepper to taste
- Chopped chives for garnish

Preparation:

1. Scramble eggs in a bowl.

2. Cook eggs in a non-stick pan until fully cooked.

3. Sprinkle Parmesan cheese over the eggs.

4. Season with salt and pepper.

5. Garnish with chopped chives.

Nutritional Value:

- Protein: 12g

- Phosphorus: < 150mg

- Potassium: < 200mg

- Sodium: < 100mg

Cooking Time:

Approximately 5 minutes.

CHAPTER 6

Lunch Recipes

1. Shrimp Noodles with Veggies

Ingredients:

- ½ cup cooked shrimp, peeled and deveined

- 1 cup cooked rice noodles

- ½ cup broccoli florets

- ¼ cup shredded carrots

- 1 tablespoon low-sodium soy sauce

- 1 teaspoon sesame oil

- Chopped green onions for garnish

Preparation:

1. Cook rice noodles according to package instructions.

2. In a pan, sauté shrimp, broccoli, and carrots until cooked.

3. Toss cooked noodles with the shrimp and vegetables.

4. Drizzle with soy sauce and sesame oil.

5. Garnish with chopped green onions.

Nutritional Value:

- Protein: 15g

- Phosphorus: < 150mg

- Potassium: < 200mg

- Sodium: < 200mg

Cooking Time:

Approximately 15 minutes.

2.   Easy Quinoa Salad

Ingredients:

- ½ cup cooked quinoa

- ¼ cup diced cucumber

- ¼ cup cherry tomatoes, halved

- ¼ cup bell peppers, diced

- 1 tablespoon olive oil

- 1 tablespoon balsamic vinegar

- Fresh basil for garnish

Preparation:

1. In a bowl, combine cooked quinoa, cucumber, tomatoes, and bell peppers.

2. Drizzle with olive oil and balsamic vinegar.

3. Toss the ingredients until well combined.

4. Garnish with fresh basil.

Nutritional Value:

- Protein: 7g

- Phosphorus: < 100mg

- Potassium: < 150mg

- Sodium: < 50mg

Cooking Time:

Approximately 20 minutes.

3. Cucumber Bites Stuffed with Chicken

- 1 cucumber, sliced into rounds
- ½ cup shredded cooked chicken breast
- 2 tablespoons Greek yogurt
- 1 tablespoon fresh dill, chopped
- Salt and pepper to taste

Preparation:

1. In a bowl, mix shredded chicken with Greek yogurt and chopped dill.

2. Season with salt and pepper.

3. Spoon the chicken mixture onto cucumber rounds.

Nutritional Value:

- Protein: 15g

- Phosphorus: < 150mg

- Potassium: < 100mg

- Sodium: < 100mg

Cooking Time:

No cooking required.

4. Fresh Pasta Salad with Vegetables

Ingredients:

- ½ cup cooked whole wheat pasta
- ¼ cup cherry tomatoes, halved
- ¼ cup cucumber, diced
- ¼ cup black olives, sliced
- 1 tablespoon olive oil
- 1 tablespoon balsamic vinegar
- Fresh parsley for garnish

Preparation:

1. Combine cooked pasta, cherry tomatoes, cucumber, and olives in a bowl.
2. Drizzle with olive oil and balsamic vinegar.
3. Toss until well coated.
4. Garnish with fresh parsley.

Nutritional Value:

- Protein: 5g

- Phosphorus: < 100mg

- Potassium: < 150mg

- Sodium: < 100mg

Cooking Time:

Approximately 15 minutes.

5.   Fusilli Salad with Avocado

- ½ cup cooked fusilli pasta
- ¼ cup diced avocado
- ¼ cup cherry tomatoes, halved
- ¼ cup red bell pepper, diced
- 1 tablespoon lemon juice
- 1 tablespoon olive oil
- Fresh cilantro for garnish

Preparation:

1. In a bowl, mix cooked fusilli pasta, avocado, tomatoes, and red bell pepper.
2. Add a drizzle of olive oil and lemon juice.
3. Toss until well combined.
4. Garnish with fresh cilantro.

Nutritional Value:

- Protein: 4g

- Phosphorus: < 100mg

- Potassium: < 200mg

- Sodium: < 50mg

Cooking Time:

Approximately 15 minutes.

6. Delicious Cod Sandwich

- ½ cup cooked cod fillet

- 1 whole grain bun

- 1 tablespoon tartar sauce (low sodium)

- Lettuce and tomato slices for garnish

1. Place cooked cod fillet on a whole grain bun.

2. Spread tartar sauce on the bun.

3. Garnish with lettuce and tomato slices.

- Protein: 20g

- Phosphorus: < 150mg

- Potassium: < 200mg

- Sodium: < 200mg

Approximately 15 minutes.

7. Tuna Salad with Feta Cheese and Spinach

Ingredients:

- ½ cup canned tuna in water, drained
- 1 cup fresh spinach
- 1 tablespoon crumbled feta cheese
- 1 tablespoon olive oil
- Lemon juice to taste
- Salt and pepper to taste

Preparation:

1. In a bowl, mix tuna, fresh spinach, and crumbled feta cheese.
2. Drizzle with olive oil and lemon juice.
3. Season with salt and pepper.

Nutritional Value:

- Protein: 20g

- Phosphorus: < 150mg

- Potassium: < 200mg

- Sodium: < 200mg

Cooking Time:

No cooking required.

8. Tasty Salmon Sandwich

Ingredients:

- ½ cup grilled salmon fillet
- 1 whole grain bun
- 1 tablespoon Greek yogurt
- 1 teaspoon Dijon mustard
- Sliced cucumber and dill for garnish

Preparation:

1. Place grilled salmon fillet on a whole grain bun.

2. Mix Greek yogurt and Dijon mustard, spread on the bun.

3. Garnish with sliced cucumber and dill.

Nutritional Value:

- Protein: 25g

- Phosphorus: < 150mg

- Potassium: < 200mg

- Sodium: < 200mg

Cooking Time:

Approximately 15 minutes.

9. Chickpea Salad with Vegetables

Ingredients:

- ½ cup canned chickpeas, drained
- ¼ cup cherry tomatoes, halved
- ¼ cup cucumber, diced
- ¼ cup red onion, finely chopped
- 1 tablespoon olive oil
- 1 tablespoon lemon juice
- Fresh parsley for garnish

Preparation:

1. In a bowl, combine chickpeas, cherry tomatoes, cucumber, and red onion.
2. Drizzle with olive oil and lemon juice.
3. Toss until well combined.
4. Garnish with fresh parsley.

Nutritional Value:

- Protein: 7g

- Phosphorus: < 100mg

- Potassium: < 150mg

- Sodium: < 100mg

Cooking Time:

No cooking required.

10. Healthy Shakshuka

Ingredients:

- 2 eggs

- ½ cup tomato sauce (low sodium)

- ¼ cup bell peppers, diced

- ¼ cup onions, diced

- 1 clove garlic, minced

- 1 teaspoon olive oil

- Salt and pepper to taste

Preparation:

1. In a pan, sauté bell peppers, onions, and garlic in olive oil until softened.

2. Add tomato sauce, season with salt and pepper.

3. Create wells in the sauce and crack eggs into them.

4. Ensure you cover and cook until eggs are done to your desired taste.

Nutritional Value:

- Protein: 14g
- Phosphorus: < 150mg
- Potassium: < 200mg
- Sodium: < 200mg

Cooking Time:

Approximately 20 minutes.

CHAPTER 7

Dinner Recipes

1. Fried Rice with Vegetables and Eggs

Ingredients:

- ½ cup cooked brown rice

- ¼ cup mixed vegetables (peas, carrots, corn)

- 1 egg, beaten

- 1 tablespoon low-sodium soy sauce

- 1 teaspoon sesame oil

- Green onions for garnish

Preparation:

1. In a pan, sauté mixed vegetables until tender.

2. Push the vegetables to one side and pour the beaten egg into the other side.

3. Scramble the egg until cooked, then mix with the vegetables.

4. Add cooked rice to the pan.

5. Drizzle with soy sauce and sesame oil, toss until well combined.

6. Garnish with green onions.

Nutritional Value:

- Protein: 10g

- Phosphorus: < 150mg

- Potassium: < 200mg

- Sodium: < 200mg

Cooking Time:

Approximately 15 minutes.

2.   Crispy Lemon Chicken

Ingredients:

- 1 boneless, skinless chicken breast
- 2 tablespoons almond flour
- 1 tablespoon lemon juice
- 1 teaspoon olive oil
- Salt, pepper, and herbs to taste

Preparation:

1. Coat the chicken breast in almond flour, salt, pepper, and herbs.

2. In a pan, heat olive oil and cook the chicken until golden and cooked through.

3. Drizzle with lemon juice before serving.

Nutritional Value:

- Protein: 25g

- Phosphorus: < 200mg

- Potassium: < 200mg

- Sodium: < 100mg

Cooking Time:

Approximately 20 minutes.

3.   Pasta with Beef

Ingredients:

- ½ cup cooked whole wheat pasta
- ¼ cup lean ground beef, cooked
- ¼ cup tomato sauce (low sodium)
- ¼ cup diced bell peppers
- 1 tablespoon olive oil
- Fresh basil for garnish

Preparation:

1. In a pan, sauté bell peppers in olive oil until softened.

2. Add cooked ground beef and tomato sauce, heat through.

3. Toss cooked pasta with the beef mixture.

4. Garnish with fresh basil.

Nutritional Value:

- Protein: 15g

- Phosphorus: < 150mg

- Potassium: < 150mg

- Sodium: < 100mg

Cooking Time:

Approximately 15 minutes.

4. Orange Flavored Tilapia

Ingredients:

- 1 tilapia fillet
- 1 tablespoon orange juice
- 1 teaspoon olive oil
- ½ teaspoon grated orange zest
- Fresh herbs (thyme or parsley) for garnish

Preparation:

1. Preheat the oven to 375°F (190°C).

2. Place tilapia fillet in a baking dish.

3. Mix orange juice, olive oil, and orange zest, then pour over the fish.

4. Bake until the fish is cooked through.

5. Garnish with fresh herbs.

Nutritional Value:

- Protein: 20g

- Phosphorus: < 150mg

- Potassium: < 200mg

- Sodium: < 100mg

Cooking Time:

Approximately 15 minutes.

5. Chicken with Mustard Sauce

Ingredients:

- 1 chicken breast
- 1 tablespoon Dijon mustard
- 1 tablespoon low-sodium chicken broth
- 1 teaspoon olive oil
- Herbs and spices to taste

Preparation:

1. Season the chicken breast with herbs and spices.

2. In a pan, heat olive oil and cook the chicken until golden and cooked through.

3. Mix Dijon mustard with chicken broth, pour over the cooked chicken.

4. Simmer until the sauce thickens.

Nutritional Value:

- Protein: 25g

- Phosphorus: < 150mg

- Potassium: < 200mg

- Sodium: < 100mg

Cooking Time:

Approximately 20 minutes.

6. Fish Sandwich with Pineapple

Ingredients:

- 1 grilled fish fillet
- 1 whole grain bun
- ¼ cup fresh pineapple slices
- Lettuce and tomato for garnish
- 1 teaspoon tartar sauce (low sodium)

Preparation:

1. Place grilled fish fillet on a whole grain bun.

2. Top with fresh pineapple slices, lettuce, and tomato.

3. Spread tartar sauce on the bun.

Nutritional Value:

- Protein: 20g

- Phosphorus: < 150mg

- Potassium: < 200mg

- Sodium: < 200mg

Cooking Time:

Approximately 15 minutes.

7. Seafood Pasta with Tomatoes

Ingredients:

- ½ cup cooked whole wheat pasta
- ¼ cup mixed seafood (shrimp, scallops)
- ¼ cup cherry tomatoes, halved
- 1 tablespoon olive oil
- 1 tablespoon lemon juice
- Fresh basil for garnish

Preparation:

1. In a pan, sauté mixed seafood until cooked.

2. Add cherry tomatoes and cook until softened.

3. Toss cooked pasta with seafood and tomatoes.

4. Drizzle with olive oil and lemon juice.

5. Garnish with fresh basil.

Nutritional Value:

- Protein: 15g

- Phosphorus: < 150mg

- Potassium: < 150mg

- Sodium: < 100mg

Cooking Time:

Approximately 15 minutes.

8. Squash with Meat Filling

Ingredients:

- 1 medium-sized squash (zucchini or yellow squash)
- ¼ cup lean ground meat (turkey or chicken)
- ¼ cup diced bell peppers
- ¼ cup diced onions
- 1 tablespoon olive oil
- Herbs and spices to taste

Preparation:

1. Cut the squash in half, scoop out the seeds.
2. In a pan, sauté ground meat, bell peppers, and onions in olive oil.
3. Season with herbs and spices.
4. Stuff the squash halves with the meat filling.
5. Bake until the squash is tender.

Nutritional Value:

- Protein: 15g

- Phosphorus: < 150mg

- Potassium: < 200mg

- Sodium: < 100mg

Cooking Time:

Approximately 30 minutes.

9.   Herb Cauliflower Rice

Ingredients:

- 1 cup cauliflower rice

- 1 tablespoon olive oil

- Fresh herbs (parsley, thyme) chopped

- Salt and pepper to taste

Preparation:

1. In a pan, heat olive oil.

2. Add cauliflower rice and sauté until tender.

3. Mix in fresh herbs, salt, and pepper.

Nutritional Value:

- Protein: 3g

- Phosphorus: < 50mg

- Potassium: < 150mg

- Sodium: < 50mg

Cooking Time:

Approximately 10 minutes.

10. Greek Style Stuffed Mushrooms

Ingredients:

- 4 large mushrooms, cleaned and stems removed

- ¼ cup feta cheese, crumbled

- ¼ cup spinach, chopped

- 1 tablespoon olive oil

- 1 teaspoon lemon juice

- Herbs and spices to taste

Preparation:

1. Preheat the oven to 375°F (190°C).

2. In a bowl, mix feta cheese, chopped spinach, olive oil, lemon juice, and seasonings.

3. Stuff each mushroom with the mixture.

4. Bake until mushrooms are tender.

Nutritional Value:

- Protein: 5g

- Phosphorus: < 100mg

- Potassium: < 200mg

- Sodium: < 100mg

Cooking Time:

Approximately 15 minutes.

CHAPTER 8

Snack Recipes

1. Vegetable Crudité Platter

Ingredients:

- 1 cup cucumber, sliced

- 1 cup cherry tomatoes

- 1 cup bell pepper strips

- 1 cup carrot sticks

- 2 tablespoons hummus (low sodium)

Preparation:

1. Arrange cucumber slices, cherry tomatoes, bell pepper strips, and carrot sticks on a platter.

2. Serve with a side of low-sodium hummus for dipping.

Nutritional Value:

- Protein: 4g

- Phosphorus: < 100mg

- Potassium: < 200mg

- Sodium: < 100mg

Preparation Time:

Approximately 10 minutes.

2.   Cottage Cheese and Fruit Bowl

Ingredients:

- ½ cup low-fat cottage cheese
- ½ cup diced melon (cantaloupe, honeydew)
- ½ cup berries (blueberries, strawberries)

Preparation:

1.   In a bowl, combine cottage cheese, diced melon, and berries.

Nutritional Value:

- Protein: 15g
- Phosphorus: < 150mg
- Potassium: < 150mg
- Sodium: < 100mg

Preparation Time:

Approximately 5 minutes.

3.   Baked Sweet Potato Chips

Ingredients:

- 1 medium sweet potato, thinly sliced
- 1 tablespoon olive oil
- Salt and pepper to taste

Preparation:

1. Preheat the oven to 375°F (190°C).
2. Toss sweet potato slices with olive oil, salt, and pepper.
3. Place on a baking sheet in a single layer.
4. Bake until crispy, flipping halfway.

Nutritional Value:

- Protein: 2g

- Phosphorus: < 50mg

- Potassium: < 200mg

- Sodium: < 50mg

Preparation Time:

Approximately 20 minutes.

4.   Quinoa Salad Cups

Ingredients:

- ½ cup cooked quinoa
- ¼ cup diced cucumber
- ¼ cup cherry tomatoes, halved
- 1 tablespoon olive oil
- Fresh herbs (parsley, mint) for garnish

Preparation:

1. In a bowl, mix cooked quinoa, diced cucumber, and cherry tomatoes.
2. Drizzle with olive oil.
3. Spoon the mixture into small cups.
4. Garnish with fresh herbs.

Nutritional Value:

- Protein: 7g

- Phosphorus: < 100mg

- Potassium: < 150mg

- Sodium: < 50mg

Preparation Time:

Approximately 15 minutes.

5. Watermelon and Feta Skewers

Ingredients:

- 1 cup watermelon, cubed
- ¼ cup feta cheese, cubed
- Fresh mint leaves
- Balsamic glaze for drizzling

Preparation:

1. Thread watermelon cubes, feta cheese, and mint leaves onto skewers.

2. Drizzle with balsamic glaze before serving.

Nutritional Value:

- Protein: 5g

- Phosphorus: < 100mg

- Potassium: < 200mg

- Sodium: < 100mg

Preparation Time:

Approximately 10 minutes.

6. Apple and Almond Butter Wraps

Ingredients:

- 1 medium apple, thinly sliced
- 2 tablespoons almond butter (unsalted)
- 1 whole grain tortilla

Preparation:

1. Spread almond butter on the whole grain tortilla.
2. Place apple slices on one side of the tortilla.
3. Roll it up and slice into bite-sized pieces.

- Protein: 5g

- Phosphorus: < 100mg

- Potassium: < 150mg

- Sodium: < 50mg

Approximately 5 minutes.

7. Melon and Prosciutto Roll-Ups

Ingredients:

- 1 cup melon balls (cantaloupe, honeydew)
- 4 slices prosciutto, cut in half

Preparation:

1.   Wrap each melon ball with a half-slice of prosciutto.

Nutritional Value:

- Protein: 10g
- Phosphorus: < 100mg
- Potassium: < 200mg
- Sodium: < 200mg

Preparation Time:

Approximately 10 minutes.

8.   Caprese Skewers

- 1 cup cherry tomatoes
- ½ cup fresh mozzarella balls
- Fresh basil leaves
- Balsamic glaze for drizzling

Preparation:

1. Thread cherry tomatoes, fresh mozzarella balls, and basil leaves onto skewers.
2. Drizzle with balsamic glaze before serving.

Nutritional Value:

- Protein: 10g
- Phosphorus: < 100mg
- Potassium: < 200mg
- Sodium: < 100mg

Preparation Time:

Approximately 10 minutes.

9. Baked Zucchini Chips

Ingredients:

- 1 medium zucchini, thinly sliced

- 1 tablespoon olive oil

- Parmesan cheese (optional)

- Salt and pepper to taste

Preparation:

1. Preheat the oven to 375°F (190°C).

2. Toss zucchini slices with olive oil, salt, and pepper.

3. Place on a baking sheet in a single layer.

4. Bake until golden and crispy.

Nutritional Value:

- Protein: 3g

- Phosphorus: < 50mg

- Potassium: < 200mg

- Sodium: < 50mg

Preparation Time:

Approximately 20 minutes.

10. Yogurt and Berry Popsicles

Ingredients:

- 1 cup low-fat yogurt
- ½ cup mixed berries (blueberries, strawberries)

Preparation:

1. In a bowl, mix yogurt and mixed berries.
2. Spoon the mixture into popsicle molds.
3. Freeze until solid.

Nutritional Value:

- Protein: 10g
- Phosphorus: < 100mg
- Potassium: < 150mg
- Sodium: < 50mg

Preparation Time:

Approximately 5 minutes plus freezing time.

CHAPTER 9

Dessert Recipes

1. Fresh Cherry Sorbet

Ingredients:

- 2 cups fresh cherries, pitted

- ¼ cup water

- 1-2 tablespoons honey or sweetener of choice

Preparation:

1. Blend fresh cherries and water until smooth.

2. Strain to remove pulp if desired.

3. Sweeten with honey or preferred sweetener.

4. Pour into a shallow dish and freeze, stirring every 30 minutes until set.

Nutritional Value:

- Protein: 1g

- Phosphorus: < 50mg

- Potassium: < 150mg

- Sodium: < 5mg

Cooking/Freezing Time:

Approximately 4 hours.

2. Super Nutritious Protein Bars

- 1 cup rolled oats
- ½ cup protein powder (low phosphorus)
- ¼ cup almond butter (unsalted)
- ¼ cup honey
- ¼ cup chopped nuts or seeds
- ¼ cup dried fruit (e.g., raisins)

Preparation:

1. Mix oats, protein powder, almond butter, honey, nuts/seeds, and dried fruit in a bowl.

2. Press the mixture into a lined pan and refrigerate until set.

3. Cut into bars before serving.

Nutritional Value:

- Protein: 10g

- Phosphorus: < 100mg

- Potassium: < 150mg

- Sodium: < 50mg

Preparation Time:

Approximately 15 minutes.

3. Coconut Lemon Cookies

- 1 cup shredded coconut

- ½ cup almond flour

- ¼ cup coconut oil, melted

- Zest of one lemon

- 2 tablespoons honey

- 1 teaspoon vanilla extract

Preparation:

1. Preheat oven to 350°F (180°C).

2. Mix shredded coconut, almond flour, melted coconut oil, lemon zest, honey, and vanilla extract.

3. Form into cookies on a lined baking sheet.

4. Bake until edges are golden.

Nutritional Value:

- Protein: 3g

- Phosphorus: < 50mg

- Potassium: < 50mg

- Sodium: < 5mg

Cooking Time:

Approximately 10-12 minutes.

4. Mini Strawberry Cheesecakes

Ingredients:

- 1 cup low-fat cream cheese
- ¼ cup Greek yogurt
- ¼ cup honey
- 1 teaspoon vanilla extract
- Mini graham cracker crusts
- Fresh strawberries for topping

Preparation:

1. In a bowl, mix cream cheese, Greek yogurt, honey, and vanilla extract until smooth.
2. Spoon the mixture into mini graham cracker crusts.
3. Top with fresh strawberries.
4. Refrigerate until set.

Nutritional Value:

- Protein: 5g

- Phosphorus: < 100mg

- Potassium: < 100mg

- Sodium: < 50mg

Preparation Time:

Approximately 2 hours (chilling time).

5.   Chocolate Banana Morsels

Ingredients:

- 2 ripe bananas, mashed
- ¼ cup cocoa powder
- ¼ cup chopped nuts or seeds
- ¼ cup shredded coconut (unsweetened)

Preparation:

1. Mix mashed bananas, cocoa powder, chopped nuts/seeds, and shredded coconut.
2. Drop spoonfuls onto a lined tray.
3. Freeze until firm.

Nutritional Value:

- Protein: 3g

- Phosphorus: < 50mg

- Potassium: < 200mg

- Sodium: < 5mg

Cooking/Freezing Time:

Approximately 2 hours.

6. Super Light Chocolate Cookies

Ingredients:

- 1 cup oat flour
- ¼ cup cocoa powder
- ¼ cup coconut oil, melted
- ¼ cup honey
- 1 teaspoon vanilla extract
- ¼ cup dark chocolate chips

Preparation:

1. Preheat oven to 350°F (180°C).

2. Mix oat flour, cocoa powder, melted coconut oil, honey, vanilla extract, and chocolate chips.

3. Form into cookies on a lined baking sheet.

4. Bake until edges are set.

Nutritional Value:

- Protein: 4g

- Phosphorus: < 50mg

- Potassium: < 50mg

- Sodium: < 5mg

Cooking Time:

Approximately 10-12 minutes.

7.   Cranberry Morsels

Ingredients:

- ½ cup dried cranberries (low sugar)

- ¼ cup almonds, finely chopped

- ¼ cup shredded coconut (unsweetened)

- 1 tablespoon honey

- ¼ teaspoon vanilla extract

Preparation:

1. Combine dried cranberries, chopped almonds, shredded coconut, honey, and vanilla extract.

2. Form into bite-sized morsels.

Nutritional Value:

- Protein: 2g

- Phosphorus: < 50mg

- Potassium: < 50mg

- Sodium: < 5mg

Preparation Time:

Approximately 10 minutes.

8. Coconut and Chocolate Bites

Ingredients:

- ½ cup shredded coconut (unsweetened)
- ¼ cup coconut oil, melted
- 2 tablespoons cocoa powder
- 1 tablespoon honey

Preparation:

1. Mix shredded coconut, melted coconut oil, cocoa powder, and honey.
2. Form into bite-sized balls.
3. Freeze until firm.

Nutritional Value:

- Protein: 2g

- Phosphorus: < 50mg

- Potassium: < 50mg

- Sodium: < 5mg

Cooking/Freezing Time:

Approximately 2 hours.

9.   Strawberry Cupcakes

Ingredients:

- 1 cup almond flour

- ¼ cup coconut flour

- ¼ cup coconut oil, melted

- ¼ cup honey

- 2 eggs

- ½ cup diced strawberries

Preparation:

1. Preheat oven to 350°F (180°C).

2. Mix almond flour, coconut flour, melted coconut oil, honey, eggs, and diced strawberries.

3. Spoon into cupcake liners.

4. Ensure you bake until a toothpick comes out clean.

Nutritional Value:

- Protein: 5g

- Phosphorus: < 100mg

- Potassium: < 100mg

- Sodium: < 50mg

Cooking Time:

Approximately 20 minutes.

10. Delicious Caramel Coated Apples

Ingredients:

- 2 apples, sliced
- ¼ cup caramel sauce (low sugar)
- Chopped nuts for coating (optional)

Preparation:

1. Dip apple slices into caramel sauce.

2. Optionally coat with chopped nuts.

3. Place on a tray and refrigerate until caramel is set.

Nutritional Value:

- Protein: 1g

- Phosphorus: < 50mg

- Potassium: < 100mg

- Sodium: < 50mg

Preparation Time:

Approximately 1 hour.

30 Day Meal Plan

Week 1

Day 1:

Breakfast: Burrito with Turkey

Lunch: Shrimp Noodles with Veggies

Dinner: Fried Rice with Vegetables and Eggs

Snack: Vegetable Crudité Platter

Dessert: Fresh Cherry Sorbet

Day 2:

Breakfast: Easy Pancakes with Fresh Fruit

Lunch: Easy Quinoa Salad

Dinner: Crispy Lemon Chicken

Snack: Cottage Cheese and Fruit Bowl

Dessert: Super Nutritious Protein Bars

Day 3:

Breakfast: Baked Eggs with Veggies

Lunch: Cucumber Bites Stuffed with Chicken

Dinner: Pasta with Beef

Snack: Baked Sweet Potato Chips

Dessert: Coconut Lemon Cookies

Day 4:

Breakfast: Toast with Avocado and Eggs

Lunch: Fresh Pasta Salad with Vegetables

Dinner: Orange Flavored Tilapia

Snack: Quinoa Salad Cups

Dessert: Mini Strawberry Cheesecakes

Day 5:

Breakfast: Fresh Fruit Salad

Lunch: Fusilli Salad with Avocado

Dinner: Chicken with Mustard Sauce

Snack: Watermelon and Feta Skewers

Dessert: Chocolate Banana Morsels

Day 6:

Breakfast: Filled Cookies

Lunch: Delicious Cod Sandwich

Dinner: Fish Sandwich with Pineapple

Snack: Apple and Almond Butter Wraps

Dessert: Super Light Chocolate Cookies

Day 7:

Breakfast: Quick and Tasty Chocolate Banana Oatmeal

Lunch: Tuna Salad with Feta Cheese and Spinach

Dinner: Seafood Pasta with Tomatoes

Snack: Melon and Prosciutto Roll-Ups

Dessert: Cranberry Morsels

Week 2

Day 8:

Breakfast: Toast with Figs and Cottage Cheese

Lunch: Tasty Salmon Sandwich

Dinner: Squash with Meat Filling

Snack: Caprese Skewers

Dessert: Coconut and Chocolate Bites

Day 9:

Breakfast: Blueberry and Oat Cake

Lunch: Chickpea Salad with Vegetables

Dinner: Herb Cauliflower Rice

Snack: Baked Zucchini Chips

Dessert: Strawberry Cupcakes

Day 10:

Breakfast: Eggs with Parmesan Cheese

Lunch: Healthy Shakshuka

Dinner: Greek Style Stuffed Mushrooms

Snack: Yogurt and Berry Popsicles

Dessert: Delicious Caramel Coated Apples

Day 11:

Breakfast: Filled Cookies

Lunch: Delicious Cod Sandwich

Dinner: Fish Sandwich with Pineapple

Snack: Apple and Almond Butter Wraps

Dessert: Super Light Chocolate Cookies

Day 12:

Breakfast: Quick and Tasty Chocolate Banana Oatmeal

Lunch: Tuna Salad with Feta Cheese and Spinach

Dinner: Seafood Pasta with Tomatoes

Snack: Melon and Prosciutto Roll-Ups

Dessert: Cranberry Morsels

Day 13:

Breakfast: Toast with Figs and Cottage Cheese

Lunch: Tasty Salmon Sandwich

Dinner: Squash with Meat Filling

Snack: Caprese Skewers

Dessert: Coconut and Chocolate Bites

Day 14:

Breakfast: Blueberry and Oat Cake

Lunch: Chickpea Salad with Vegetables

Dinner: Herb Cauliflower Rice

Snack: Baked Zucchini Chips

Dessert: Strawberry Cupcakes

Week 3

Breakfast: Eggs with Parmesan Cheese

Lunch: Healthy Shakshuka

Dinner: Greek Style Stuffed Mushrooms

Snack: Yogurt and Berry Popsicles

Dessert: Delicious Caramel Coated Apples

Breakfast: Burrito with Turkey

Lunch: Shrimp Noodles with Veggies

Dinner: Fried Rice with Vegetables and Eggs

Snack: Vegetable Crudité Platter

Dessert: Fresh Cherry Sorbet

Day 17:

Breakfast: Easy Pancakes with Fresh Fruit

Lunch: Easy Quinoa Salad

Dinner: Crispy Lemon Chicken

Snack: Cottage Cheese and Fruit Bowl

Dessert: Super Nutritious Protein Bars

Day 18:

Breakfast: Baked Eggs with Veggies

Lunch: Cucumber Bites Stuffed with Chicken

Dinner: Pasta with Beef

Snack: Baked Sweet Potato Chips

Dessert: Coconut Lemon Cookies

Day 19:

Breakfast: Toast with Avocado and Eggs

Lunch: Fresh Pasta Salad with Vegetables

Dinner: Orange Flavored Tilapia

Snack: Quinoa Salad Cups

Dessert: Mini Strawberry Cheesecakes

Day 20:

Breakfast: Fresh Fruit Salad

Lunch: Fusilli Salad with Avocado

Dinner: Chicken with Mustard Sauce

Snack: Watermelon and Feta Skewers

Dessert: Chocolate Banana Morsels

Day 21:

Breakfast: Baked Eggs with Veggies

Lunch: Cucumber Bites Stuffed with Chicken

Dinner: Pasta with Beef

Snack: Baked Sweet Potato Chips

Dessert: Coconut Lemon Cookies

Week 4

Day 22:

Breakfast: Quick and Tasty Chocolate Banana Oatmeal

Lunch: Tuna Salad with Feta Cheese and Spinach

Dinner: Seafood Pasta with Tomatoes

Snack: Melon and Prosciutto Roll-Ups

Dessert: Cranberry Morsels

Day 23:

Breakfast: Eggs with Parmesan Cheese

Lunch: Healthy Shakshuka

Dinner: Greek Style Stuffed Mushrooms

Snack: Yogurt and Berry Popsicles

Dessert: Delicious Caramel Coated Apples

Day 24:

Breakfast: Toast with Figs and Cottage Cheese

Lunch: Tasty Salmon Sandwich

Dinner: Squash with Meat Filling

Snack: Caprese Skewers

Dessert: Coconut and Chocolate Bites

Day 25:

Breakfast: Burrito with Turkey

Lunch: Shrimp Noodles with Veggies

Dinner: Fried Rice with Vegetables and Eggs

Snack: Vegetable Crudité Platter

Dessert: Fresh Cherry Sorbet

Day 26:

Breakfast: Toast with Avocado and Eggs

Lunch: Fresh Pasta Salad with Vegetables

Dinner: Orange Flavored Tilapia

Snack: Quinoa Salad Cups

Dessert: Mini Strawberry Cheesecakes

Day 27:

Breakfast: Filled Cookies

Lunch: Delicious Cod Sandwich

Dinner: Fish Sandwich with Pineapple

Snack: Apple and Almond Butter Wraps

Dessert: Super Light Chocolate Cookies

Day 28:

Breakfast: Blueberry and Oat Cake

Lunch: Chickpea Salad with Vegetables

Dinner: Herb Cauliflower Rice

Snack: Baked Zucchini Chips

Dessert: Strawberry Cupcakes

Day 29:

Breakfast: Fresh Fruit Salad

Lunch: Fusilli Salad with Avocado

Dinner: Chicken with Mustard Sauce

Snack: Watermelon and Feta Skewers

Dessert: Chocolate Banana Morsels

Day 30:

Breakfast: Easy Pancakes with Fresh Fruit

Lunch: Easy Quinoa Salad

Dinner: Crispy Lemon Chicken

Snack: Cottage Cheese and Fruit Bowl

Dessert: Super Nutritious Protein Bars

CONCLUSION

In conclusion, this CKD Stage 4 Cookbook for Seniors provides a thorough manual for figuring out a diet that is friendly to the kidneys while still enjoying a rich and flavorful culinary experience. With a range of recipes for breakfast, lunch, dinner, snacks, and desserts, this cookbook attempts to make meal planning easy and enjoyable for people with Stage 4 Chronic Kidney Disease.

Every recipe is carefully crafted to comply with the dietary guidelines linked with Stage 4 CKD, with a focus on reducing sodium, potassium, and phosphorus levels while ensuring a sufficient intake of protein. Nutrient-dense ingredients guarantee that seniors with kidney issues can enjoy nutritious, tasty meals that support their general health.

Remember, the choices we make today greatly affects us tomorrow. A kidney-friendly diet is a celebration of life, an affirmation of your inner strength, and a commitment to managing Stage 4 CKD. It also sends a message that your health is important. Every meal you enjoy now is a step closer to a healthier, happier future. Your quest for better health is a personal victory.

In the words of an ancient proverb, "He who has health has hope, and he who has hope has everything." So, relish in the experience, savor every bite, and allow the satisfying flavors of these recipes motivate you to live a more active and healthy lifestyle. You are cultivating the most valuable gift imaginable—your health—with every nutritious meal, proving that your well-being is worth the investment. Cheers to a kidney-friendly journey ahead!

My Little Request

Dear Reader,

Thanks for your purchase, hope you enjoyed reading.

Could you please take a few seconds to leave a positive feedback on this book?

It'll help reach more people and we can collectively help reverse this deadly disease.

Thank you.

BONUS: MEAL PLANNER JOURNAL

	BREAKFAST	LUNCH	DINNER	SNACKS
MON				
TUES				
WED				
THURS				
FRI				
SAT				
SUN				

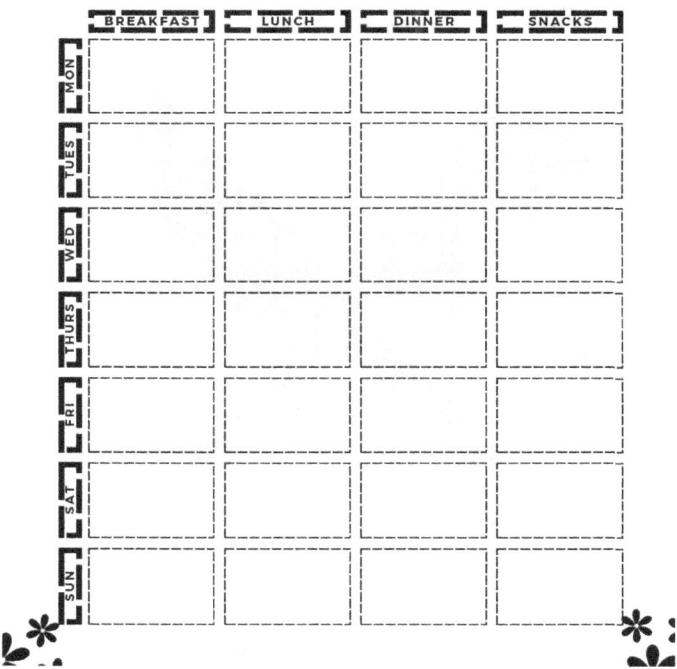

	BREAKFAST	LUNCH	DINNER	SNACKS
MON				
TUES				
WED				
THURS				
FRI				
SAT				
SUN				

	BREAKFAST	LUNCH	DINNER	SNACKS
MON				
TUES				
WED				
THURS				
FRI				
SAT				
SUN				

CKD STAGE 4 COOKBOOK FOR SENIORS

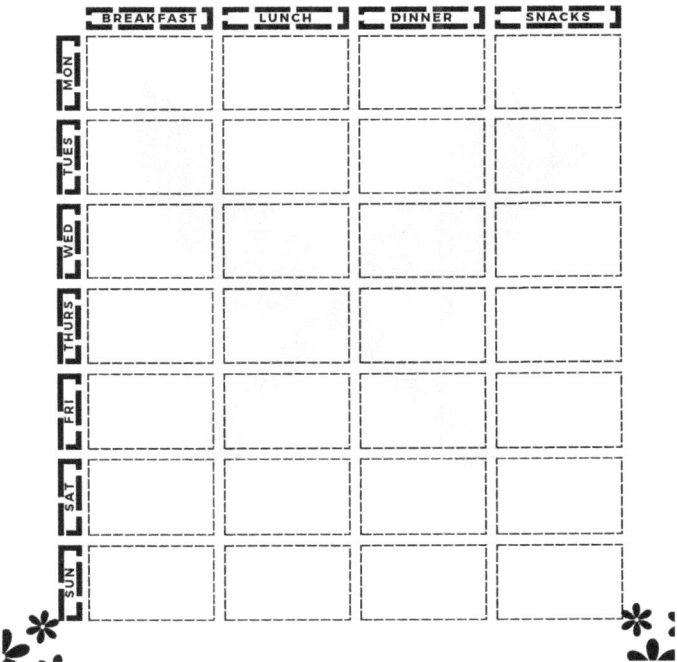

	BREAKFAST	LUNCH	DINNER	SNACKS
MON				
TUES				
WED				
THURS				
FRI				
SAT				
SUN				

WEEKLY MEAL PLANNER

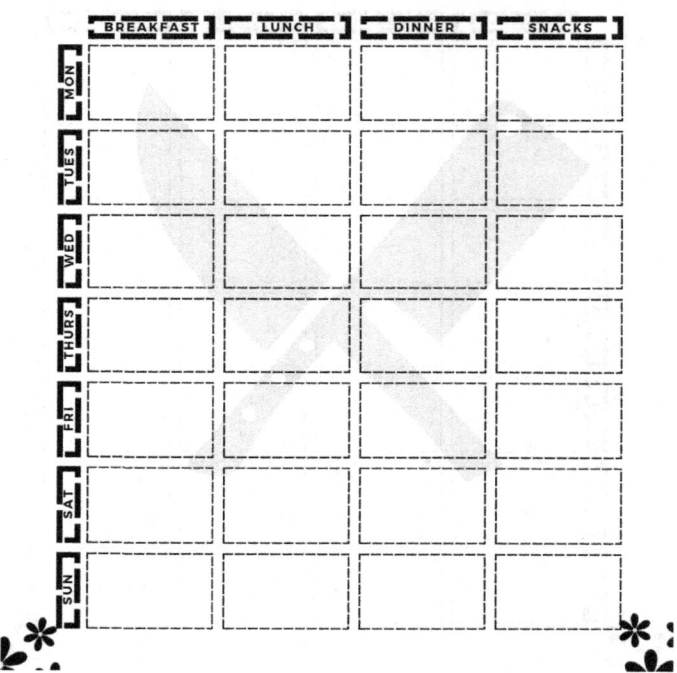

	BREAKFAST	LUNCH	DINNER	SNACKS
MON				
TUES				
WED				
THURS				
FRI				
SAT				
SUN				

WEEKLY MEAL PLANNER

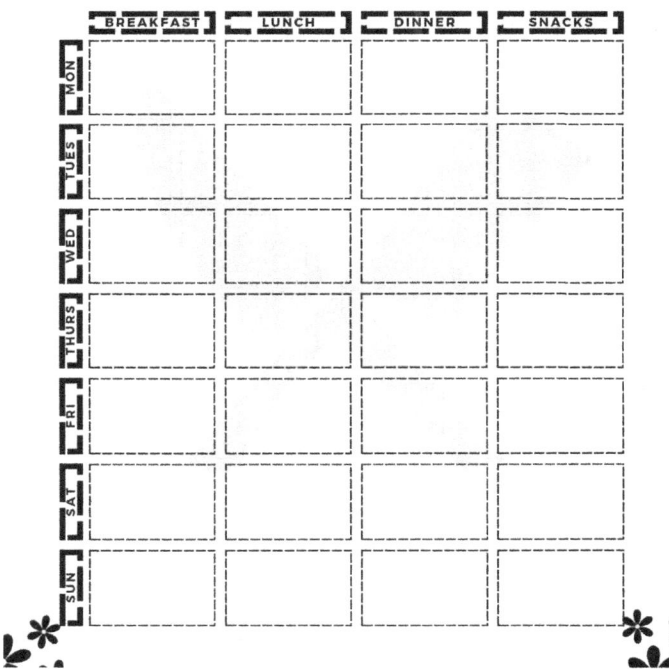

	BREAKFAST	LUNCH	DINNER	SNACKS
MON				
TUES				
WED				
THURS				
FRI				
SAT				
SUN				

WEEKLY MEAL PLANNER

	BREAKFAST	LUNCH	DINNER	SNACKS
MON				
TUES				
WED				
THURS				
FRI				
SAT				
SUN				

WEEKLY MEAL PLANNER

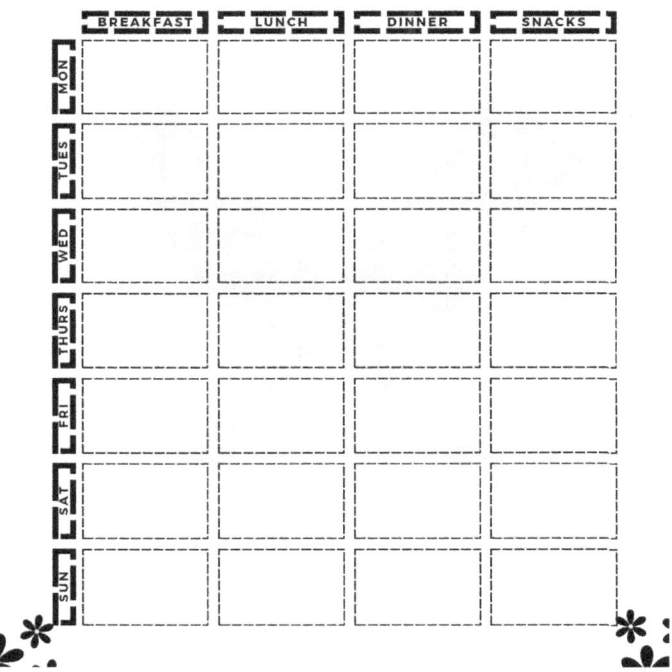

	BREAKFAST	LUNCH	DINNER	SNACKS
MON				
TUES				
WED				
THURS				
FRI				
SAT				
SUN				

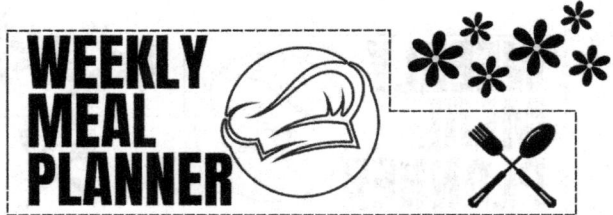

WEEKLY MEAL PLANNER

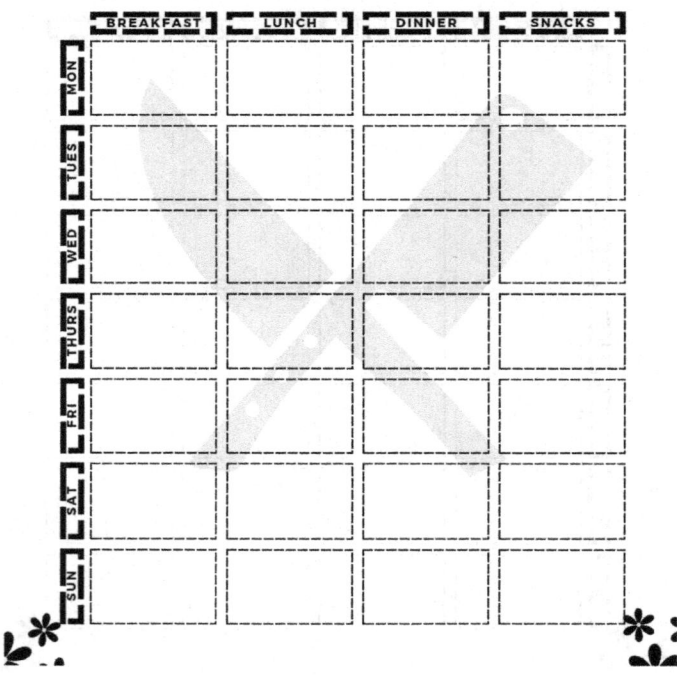

	BREAKFAST	LUNCH	DINNER	SNACKS
MON				
TUES				
WED				
THURS				
FRI				
SAT				
SUN				

	BREAKFAST	LUNCH	DINNER	SNACKS
MON				
TUES				
WED				
THURS				
FRI				
SAT				
SUN				

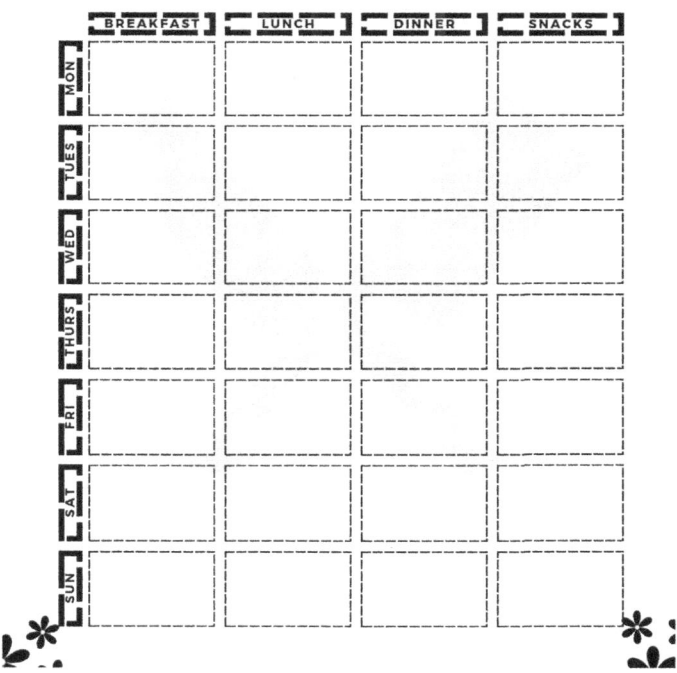

CKD STAGE 4 COOKBOOK FOR SENIORS

	BREAKFAST	LUNCH	DINNER	SNACKS
MON				
TUES				
WED				
THURS				
FRI				
SAT				
SUN				

CKD STAGE 4 COOKBOOK FOR SENIORS

	BREAKFAST	LUNCH	DINNER	SNACKS
MON				
TUES				
WED				
THURS				
FRI				
SAT				
SUN				

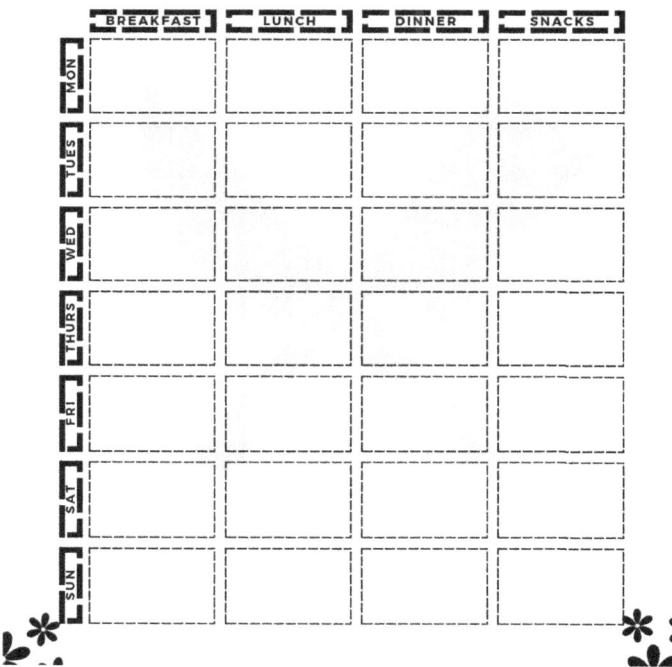

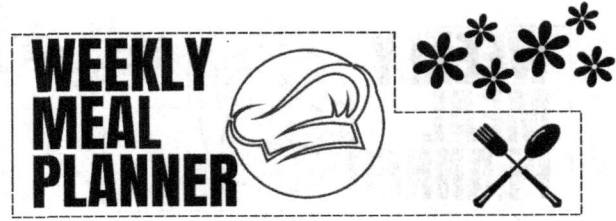

WEEKLY MEAL PLANNER

	BREAKFAST	LUNCH	DINNER	SNACKS
MON				
TUES				
WED				
THURS				
FRI				
SAT				
SUN				

WEEKLY MEAL PLANNER

	BREAKFAST	LUNCH	DINNER	SNACKS
MON				
TUES				
WED				
THURS				
FRI				
SAT				
SUN				

WEEKLY MEAL PLANNER

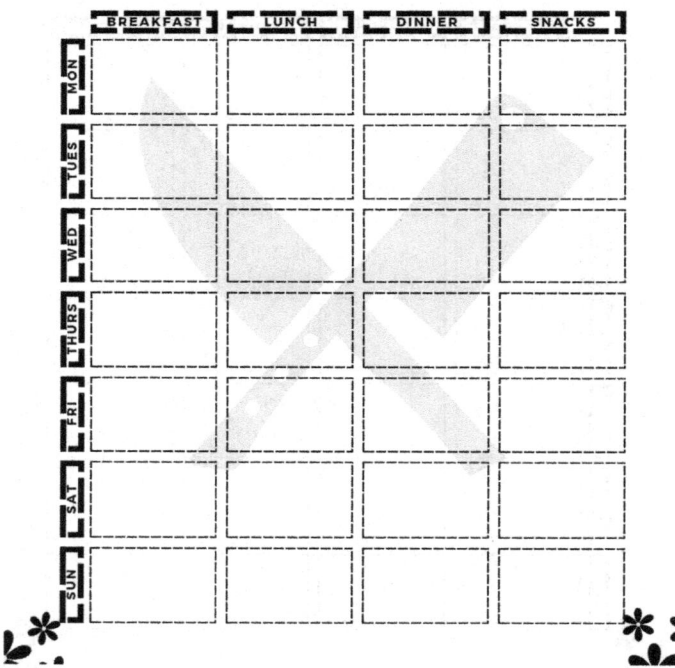

	BREAKFAST	LUNCH	DINNER	SNACKS
MON				
TUES				
WED				
THURS				
FRI				
SAT				
SUN				

	BREAKFAST	LUNCH	DINNER	SNACKS
MON				
TUES				
WED				
THURS				
FRI				
SAT				
SUN				

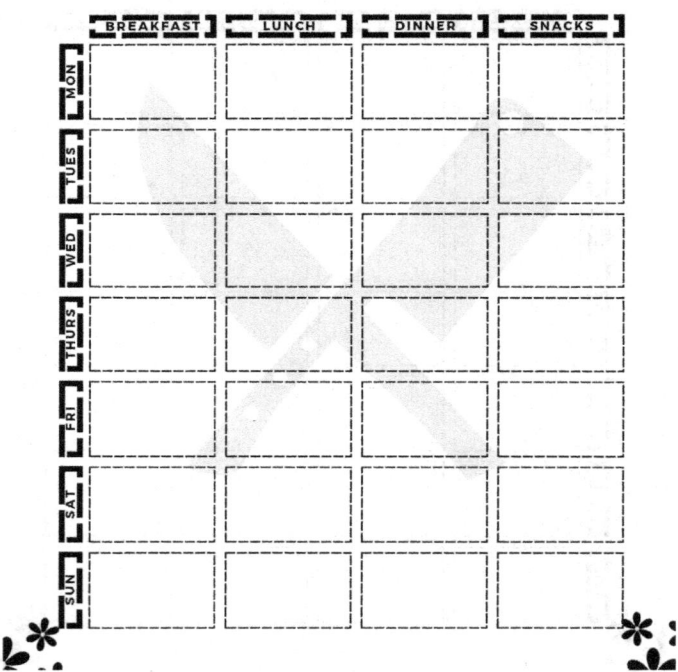

	BREAKFAST	LUNCH	DINNER	SNACKS
MON				
TUES				
WED				
THURS				
FRI				
SAT				
SUN				

	BREAKFAST	LUNCH	DINNER	SNACKS
MON				
TUES				
WED				
THURS				
FRI				
SAT				
SUN				

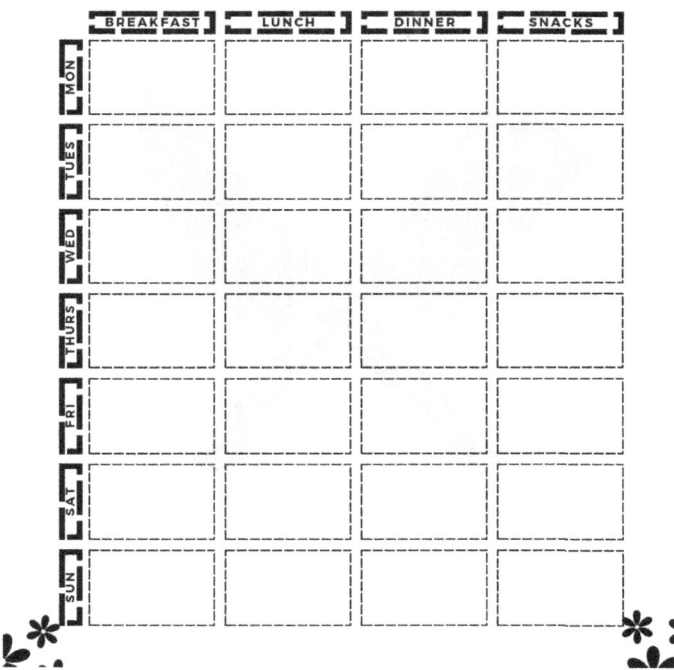

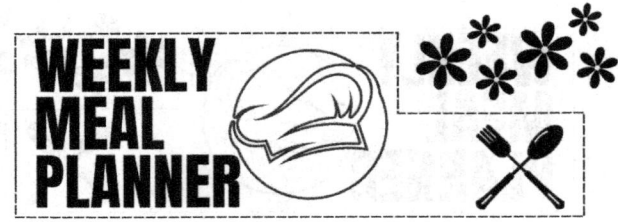

WEEKLY MEAL PLANNER

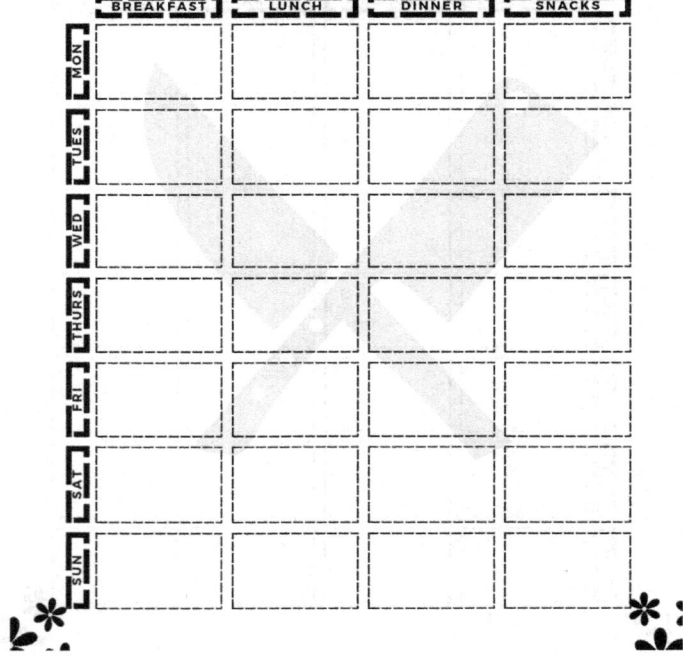

	BREAKFAST	LUNCH	DINNER	SNACKS
MON				
TUES				
WED				
THURS				
FRI				
SAT				
SUN				

WEEKLY MEAL PLANNER

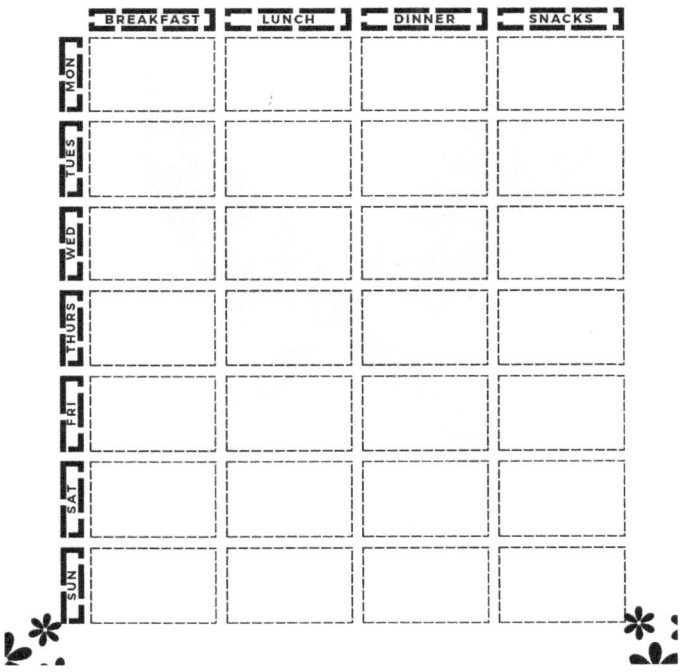

	BREAKFAST	LUNCH	DINNER	SNACKS
MON				
TUES				
WED				
THURS				
FRI				
SAT				
SUN				

	BREAKFAST	LUNCH	DINNER	SNACKS
MON				
TUES				
WED				
THURS				
FRI				
SAT				
SUN				

CKD STAGE 4 COOKBOOK FOR SENIORS

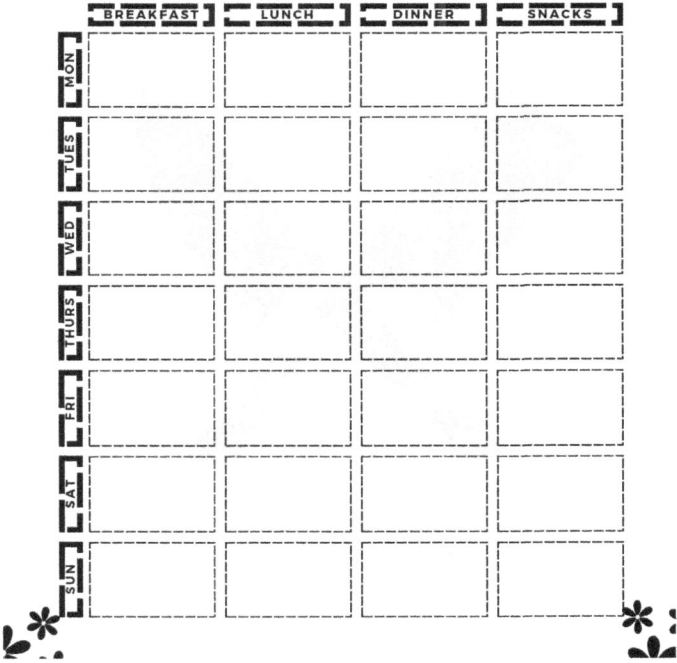

	BREAKFAST	LUNCH	DINNER	SNACKS
MON				
TUES				
WED				
THURS				
FRI				
SAT				
SUN				

CKD STAGE 4 COOKBOOK FOR SENIORS

Made in the USA
Coppell, TX
13 February 2025

45919789R00105